Marathon

Marathon

RICHARD LAYMON

GLOBE FEARON
Pearson Learning Group

FASTBACK® SPORTS BOOKS

ISBN 0-13-024603-4

Printed in the United States of America

1 2 3 4 5 6 7 8 9 10   07 06 05 04 03

Globe
Fearon

Pearson Learning Group

1-800-321-3106
www.pearsonlearning.com

"Claymore," the official said, "you're number forty-six." He checked Rod Claymore's name on the entry sheet next to the number, and gave him a square patch of cloth marked "46." "Good luck, Claymore."

Rod nodded and stepped out of the way. He took four safety pins from a card table nearby, then crossed the track to the grassy infield. There, he pinned the number to the front of his running shirt.

He found a clear area, sat on the ground, and worked on stretching exercises.

Except for his stomach, he felt good. His stomach felt tight and jittery. Ever since signing up for the marathon, two months ago, he had looked forward to this day with the same dread as if waiting for a visit to the dentist. But this would be far worse than any dental appointment. This would be a killer. Marathons always were.

This would be his seventh. He knew how it would be. He would run the 26 miles and 385 yards in two hours and fifteen minutes—maybe faster today—and spend the next two months suffering from it.

To those who weren't long-distance runners, it seemed insane. Sometimes, it even seemed crazy to Rod. Why should he put himself through such pain? He always had the same answer. Because the marathon is the greatest test of a runner. Simply to finish a race of that length was a real victory. To win, to break the tape first in a group of 50 or 100 runners, was a thrill that couldn't be matched.

He had won his last two marathons. He planned to win this one.

Raising his head, he looked at the stadium stands. Without a doubt, few in the crowd had ever heard of Rod Claymore. Many probably had hometown favorites, but Rod was just another stranger to most of them. Two and a half hours from now, however, they would all be on their feet and cheering him, as he entered the stadium ahead of all the others. The announcer's voice would boom over the loud speakers, "That's forty-six, folks! Rod Claymore!" He wouldn't be just another nameless stranger anymore. He would be the winner. And that would make it worth the pain.

He leaned forward, face to his knees, and grabbed the soles of his shoes. He felt loose. He felt fine. He knew the butterflies in his stomach would go away at the blast of the starting gun.

"Howdy," someone said.

Rod sat up and nodded at a lean young man who looked about seventeen. The number "32" was pinned to his shirt. He had red hair. His face was spotted with freckles. "Hi there," Rod said.

"I'm Austin." Stepping closer, he bent down and put out his hand. Rod shook it. "Austin Henry. Mostly, they call me Tex."

"How're you doing, Tex? I'm Rod Claymore. Mostly, they call me collect."

Tex laughed, but his eyes kept their nervous look. He, too, was probably dreading the race. "You from these parts?" he asked.

"Oregon. I'll make a bet you're from the

Longhorn State," Rod said, smiling.

"That's me," Tex said.

"You're a long way from home."

"Well, sir, this is a big race for me. I figure it's worth the trip, as long as I win it. And I sure don't aim to lose."

"You'll have to settle for second, pardner."

"Second won't cut it," Tex said.

"Have you ever won a marathon?" Rod asked.

"Nope. I came in second in Dallas last year, but since then I've knocked a couple of minutes off my time. So I'm figuring to win this one."

"Good luck," Rod said. "You'll need it."

"The way I see things, it's not a question of luck. It's just guts. The winner's the guy who wants to win more than the rest of them. And that's me."

"Did you bring along your six-gun, Tex?"

He made a lopsided grin. "No, I left it home."

"Too bad. If you were packing it, you could've plugged me in the back and had a chance."

Tex laughed. "Know what? You're a little nuts, Rod."

Rod laughed, too.

A voice on the loud speakers told the runners to take their positions.

Tex's face turned a little pale. "I guess this is it," he said. He rubbed his hands on his shorts.

Rod got to his feet. He held out a hand,

and Tex shook it. "Have a good one," Rod said.

Then they walked onto the track and joined the crowd of runners. A few nodded greetings.

Rod took deep breaths. He touched his toes. The day was warm, but a blanket of clouds hid the sun. There seemed to be a slight breeze.

"To your marks."

Silence fell over the stadium. Rod braced himself. He glanced at Tex. The kid was wiping sweat off his face.

"Get set."

Here goes, he thought. His stomach felt knotted.

The starting gun sounded and more than 100 runners were off.

Rod took off slowly. He stayed near the middle of the pack as it circled the stadium track. Tex, he saw, was a short distance ahead. From the way the kid had talked, Rod thought he might rush out to take the lead. That would have been a bad mistake.

If this race went like most, those starting at the front would quickly wear out and finish far behind the ones smart enough to hold back. You always try to keep the leaders in sight. But you stick to your own pace and save your big push for the last third of the race.

Rod jogged along easily. After two laps of the track, the runners made their way through a tunnel and left the stadium behind them. A scattering of people cheered from the sidewalks. He stayed near the right-hand curb. Many other runners spread out across the street as if they didn't know or care that, four blocks ahead, they would have to come back to this side for a turn. They were wasting steps, making the race all the longer for themselves.

Tex, however, stayed close to the right. *He knows his stuff,* Rod thought.

Tex made the turn half a block ahead of him.

During the next several miles, the cluster of runners thinned out, forming a narrow line that stretched far in front of Rod. The line was probably even longer behind him, but he didn't look back. That would use up energy. Also, a moment to glance over the shoulder was a moment he might step on something, turn his ankle, fall. Even a small injury, at any point along the route, could cost him the race. So he kept his eyes forward.

He didn't worry about the runners in front of him. He worried only about keeping his own steady pace. Sooner or later, he would overtake most of them without speeding up. They would simply lose steam and slow down.

Mile after mile, it worked that way. Though a few runners came up from behind Rod and passed him, a much greater number dropped back. Even the leader, near the middle of the street two blocks ahead, slowed to a stagger before the runners reached the halfway mark.

Tex, with his red hair, yellow shirt, and bright green shorts, took over fourth place.

Not bad, Rod thought. He wondered how soon Tex would poop out.

Maybe he won't.

For the next mile, the road slanted uphill. Rod leaned into it. He chugged along, keeping his pace, but the slope was bad. It drained his strength. He blinked sweat out of his eyes.

Look on the bright side, he told himself. *It's getting them, too.*

On the uphill, he passed six more runners. One, who had been trailing Tex by a few yards, stumbled off the road and lay down on the sidewalk. He was crying, as Rod jogged past.

Finally, the road leveled out.

Rod counted ten runners ahead of him. Tex, now in third place, seemed in no hurry to try for the lead. He was two long blocks ahead of Rod.

Rod angled slowly to the left, planning to reach the far corner just in time for the turn onto Washington Boulevard.

The turn would mark the two-thirds point in the race. Seventeen miles down, nine to go.

He rounded the corner.

It was time to make his move.

Rod quickened his stride. His long legs reached out, eating up the pavement between him and those ahead. Some heard him coming and picked up speed to keep him from passing. Their efforts didn't last long. One after another, he left them behind. Block after block, he made his way closer to those in front.

Tex, no more than 50 yards ahead, was neck and neck with the leader. Then he was first.

Rod gained on him. He stretched out his legs, feet smacking the road, arms pumping. His lungs burned. His whole body felt like it was on fire. But he knew he could take the pain.

He raced across Palm Avenue.

Six miles to go. He could take the pain for six miles. At just over five minutes each, he would reach the finish line in a little more than half an hour. He could stand it that long. He had to.

He passed the only runner left between himself and Tex. Tex was still 30 yards ahead.

His dazed mind chanted a cheerleader yell he remembered from high school. *"You can do it, you can do it, you can, you can!"* The words pounded through his head, over and over again, with the beat of his shoes on the road.

He began to think about a stream rushing through the mountains near his home. He saw himself diving into it. He could almost feel its icy water. He could almost taste it.

Keep your mind on the race, he warned himself.

*You can do it, you can do it, you can,
you can!*

Ten yards behind Tex.

Five.

Tex looked over his shoulder.

Mistake!

Four yards.

I told you I'd win, cowboy! Rod thought
the words, but didn't say them. It hurt too
much to speak.

Tex picked up speed.

So did Rod. He chased the kid, block
after block, unable to close the gap.

At Maple Avenue, Tex took the turn
wide. Rod gained a yard on him. Now he
was only nine feet behind. Only a few
strides.

Only three miles were left in the race.
Fifteen, sixteen minutes.

A few blocks ahead, there would be another turn. *If Tex goes out wide on that one,* Rod thought, *I'll have my chance to pick up at least another yard.*

Reaching deep inside himself, Rod came up with an extra push. He drew closer and closer to Tex. The corner was just ahead. He cut toward it, lunging between the curb and Tex.

Tex didn't take it wide.

Rod's toe caught the back of Tex's foot. With a gasp, the kid clawed at the air and fell sprawling onto the road.

Rod stayed on his feet. He ran a few more steps, then looked back.

Tex, on hands and knees, was trying to stand. His left knee was bloody.

Rod staggered back to him. He grabbed Tex under one arm and helped him up. "Sorry," he gasped. "Didn't . . . mean to . . ."

Tex pulled his arm free and started to run again. His run was more like a hobble. Rod caught up to him easily. The boy's face was twisted with pain, his teeth bared in something like an awful grin. His breath came out in sobs, but there were no tears in his eyes. His eyes looked tough and stubborn.

He still thinks he can win, Rod thought.

No way. Not with his knee banged up like that. Not with almost three miles left before the finish line. Each time he put his left foot down, his face twitched. Rod could almost feel the pain himself.

Give it up, he thought.

But Tex kept limping along, his pace hardly faster than a walk.

Rod stayed beside him.

At first, they were still far ahead of the others. Rod knew he was breaking his rule about looking back, but he kept glancing over his shoulder. The first runner to come into view was a skinny guy with long, flopping blond hair. He was nearly two blocks behind when Rod spotted him.

"Pick it up," Rod said.

Tex answered with a groan.

"Come on, you can do it."

The boy's chin jutted out, and he limped along a little faster.

Behind the blond guy were three more runners, then four. He was well in front of them and picking up speed, probably gaining strength now that he had the leaders in sight. Soon, he was only a block away.

"He's . . . gonna catch us," Rod said.

"Go," Tex gasped.

Rod stayed with Tex, matching his slow strides.

Then he heard quick slapping footfalls close behind him.

He stayed with Tex.

Then the blond guy ran by him.

No way, Rod thought.

With a final glance at Tex, he went for the new leader. *I haven't come this far to give up now*, he thought.

His body felt heavy and stiff from keeping to the easy pace. His muscles and lungs acted as if the race was over. They were ready for a rest, not for more pain. But Rod forced himself onward.

The kid would have left me behind, he told himself. He kept pushing his legs forward. And he kept trying to push Tex out of his mind. *I don't even know the guy,* he thought. *Why should I feel guilty? It's every man for himself.*

Rod looked quickly over his shoulder. No other runner was close behind. He thought he saw Tex half-running, half-limping about two blocks back, but he wasn't sure. Well, the kid wasn't a quitter.

Only one guy to worry about, he thought. He tried to think only of the blond guy who was out in front. He forced himself to ignore the pain in his lungs. *Push, push, you can do it. You can catch him.*

I can't let this guy beat me, he thought. Gritting his teeth, he drove his legs out far and fast.

He knew he could catch this guy. After all, he had done it once before.

Do it again, he told himself.

You can do it.

He pumped his aching arms harder. He flung out his legs faster. His heart thundered. His lungs felt as if they'd been ripped by a knife. He heard himself make whimpering sounds, as he fought for breath.

Block after block, he chased the leader. He couldn't close the gap.

Blinking sweat from his eyes, he glimpsed a street sign. Olive Lane. Only half a mile from the stadium. Then one lap around the track inside. Three quarters of a mile left.

You can do it.

In a few minutes, it will be over.

Come on!

He forced his body to pick up speed.

Rod saw the stadium on the next block. The street outside was lined with people. They cheered the guy in front. They cheered Rod as he tried to overtake him.

Go, go, go, his mind shouted.

He gained on the leader. His fists drove at the air. His feet pounded the road.

The guy looked back.

Rod stopped. He turned around.

And started to run the other way.

People shouted at him. They waved him back. They seemed to think he had lost his sense of direction. A man in a ball cap rushed out from the curb and tried to turn him around. "*That* way," the man said, pointing back toward the stadium. "It's *that* way."

Rod pulled free of the man and started running again.

He didn't listen to the yells.

He ran toward other runners. Two of them, in a race for second place, dashed by without giving him a glance. The next one looked as if he thought Rod was crazy. The last of the four turned and

started to follow him. Maybe he thought
the rest had made a wrong turn some-
where. Rod waved him back, and kept on
running.

As he kept going in the wrong direction,
he almost laughed out loud. He was pic-
turing the confused faces of the people in
the crowd, and the other runners who
were heading for the finish. He felt like he
was driving the wrong way on a one-way
street.

He ran until he got to Tex. The kid, hob-
bling along and groaning, stared at him.

"What are you . . . ?"

"Next time," Rod gasped. "I'll beat you
next time . . . cowpoke."

The kid looked up at him and grinned
slightly. "I would have beat you *today*,"

he said weakly. "I *was* beating you," he added.

"You've never seen my closing kick, cowpoke," Rod said. I'll show you *that* next time, too."

Side by side, they slowly made their way into the stadium.